BLOOMFIELD TOWNSHIP PUBLIC LIBRARY

W9-DET-081

• BLOOMFIELD TOWNSHIP PUBLIC LIBRARY
1099 Lone Pine Road
Bloomfield Hills, Michigan 48302-2437

This is a Dorling Kindersley Book
published by Random House, Inc.

Editors Andrea Pinnington,
Charlotte Davies
Designer Heather Blackham
Managing Editor Jane Yorke
Senior Art Editor Mark Richards
Photography Steve Gorton

Additional Photography
Peter Chadwick, Philip Dowell,
Paul Goff, Frank Greenaway,
Colin Keates, Dave King, Stephen Oliver,
Kim Taylor, Jerry Young
Series Consultant Neil Morris

First American edition, 1991

Copyright © 1991 Dorling Kindersley Limited, London.
All rights reserved under International and Pan-American Copyright Conventions.
Published in the United States by Random House, Inc., New York.
This edition first published in Great Britain by
Dorling Kindersley Publishers Limited in 1991.

Library of Congress Cataloging-in-Publication Data
My first look at nature.
    p. cm.
    Originally published by Dorling Kindersley Ltd., London.
    Summary: Photographs and text depict elements of nature, such as
plants, birds, insects, and other animals, in their various natural
settings.
    ISBN 0-679-81805-7
    1. Nature – Juvenile literature. [1. Nature.] I. Random House
(Firm)
    QH48.M9 1991
    508 - dc20
    90-23568

Manufactured in Italy 1 2 3 4 5 6 7 8 9 10

Reproduced by Bright Arts, Hong Kong
Printed in Italy by L.E.G.O.

· MY · FIRST · LOOK · AT ·

Nature

BLOOMFIELD TOWNSHIP PUBLIC LIBRARY
1099 Lone Pine Road
Bloomfield Hills. Michigan 48302-2437

Random House ⌂ New York

Flowers

Flowers grow from seeds and bulbs.

petals

seeds

bud

stem

leaf

bulbs

rose

freesia

carnation

tulip

lily

delphinium

AUG 13 1992 B & TAYLOR

Mini-beasts

You can find these insects and worms in the garden.

honeybee

bumblebee

honeycomb

centipede

snail

spider

ladybugs

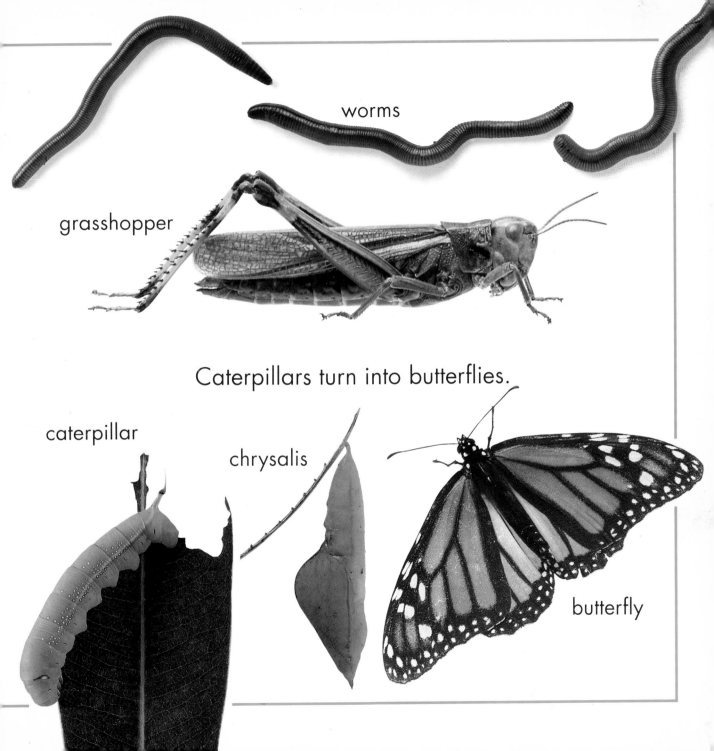

worms

grasshopper

Caterpillars turn into butterflies.

caterpillar

chrysalis

butterfly

Trees

Tiny acorns grow into tall oak trees.

acorns

horse chestnuts

berries

oak tree

maple seeds

leaves

bark

pine cone

branch

conifer

Animals

You might see these animals in towns and in the country.

lizard

squirrel

bat

mouse

snake

rabbit

Birds

Most birds lay their eggs in nests.

owl

bird's nest

birds' eggs

feathers

pheasant

sparrow

By the water

Many plants and animals live in ponds, lakes, and rivers.

water lily

duck

newt

fish

frog eggs

tadpole   dragonfly

frog

Tadpoles turn into frogs.

cattails

Along the seashore

You might see all these things at the beach.

sea horse

sea urchins

crab

sand

seaweed

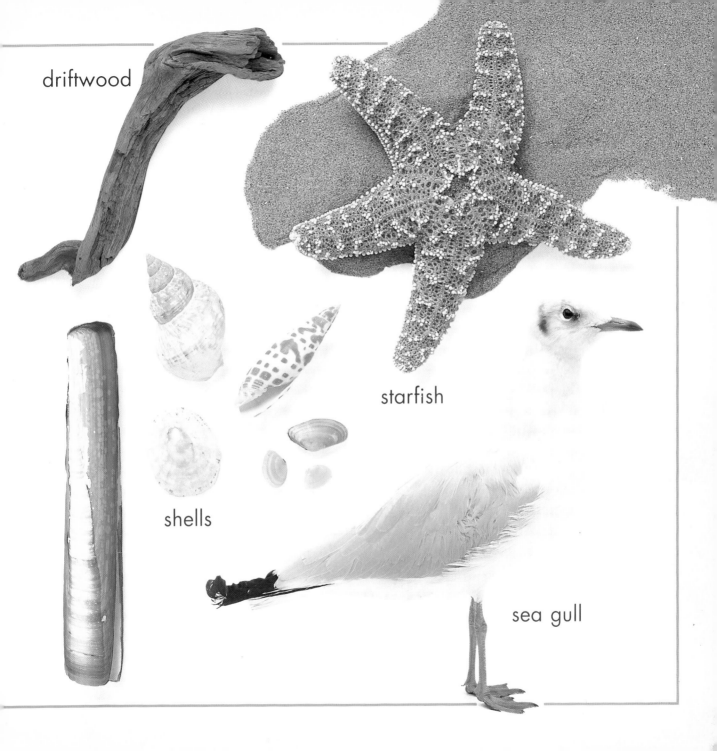

driftwood

starfish

shells

sea gull

Do you know?

What do these things grow into?

acorns

egg

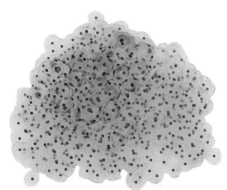

frog eggs

bulbs

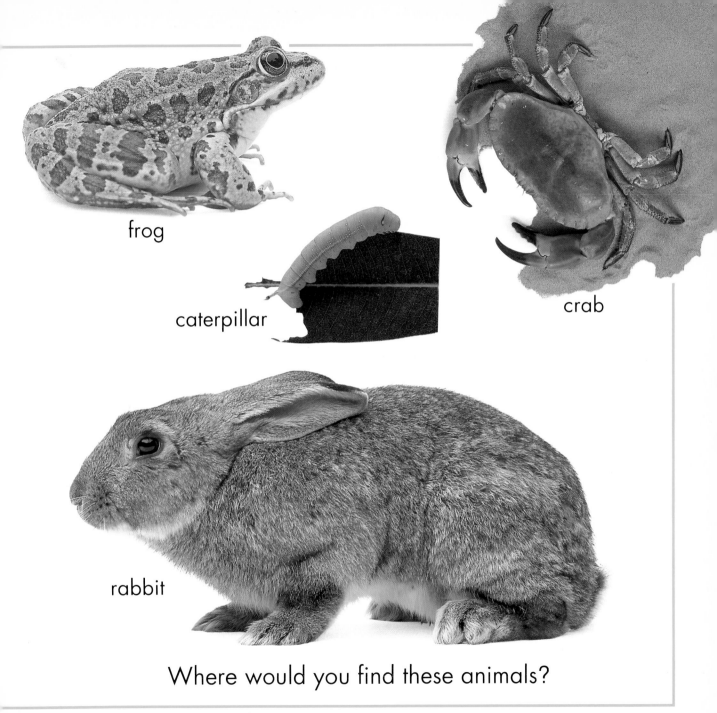

frog

caterpillar

crab

rabbit

Where would you find these animals?